OCTOPUSES
Underwater Jet Propulsion

by Andreu Llamas
Illustrated by Gabriel Casadevall and Ali Garousi

Gareth Stevens Publishing
MILWAUKEE

For a free color catalog describing Gareth Stevens' list of high-quality books and multimedia programs, call 1-800-542-2595 (USA) or 1-800-461-9120 (Canada). Gareth Stevens Publishing's Fax: (414) 225-0377.
See our catalog, too, on the World Wide Web: http://gsinc.com

The editor would like to extend special thanks to Richard Sajdak, Aquarium and Reptile Curator, Milwaukee County Zoo, Milwaukee, Wisconsin, for his kind and professional help with the information in this book.

Library of Congress Cataloging-in-Publication Data

Llamas, Andreu.
    [Pulpo. English]
    Octopuses: underwater jet propulsion / by Andreu Llamas; illustrated by Gabriel Casadevall and Ali Garousi.
       p. cm. – (Secrets of the animal world)
    Includes bibliographical references and index.
    Summary: Examines the habitat, intelligence, self-defense actions, and jet propulsion of this tentacled marine mollusk.
    ISBN 0-8368-1499-1 (lib. bdg.)
    1. Octopus–Juvenile literature. [1. Octopus.] I. Casadevall, Gabriel, ill. II. Garousi, Ali, ill. III. Title. IV. Series.
QL430.3.02L5813   1996
594'.56–dc20   95-26824

This North American edition first published in 1996 by
Gareth Stevens Publishing
1555 North RiverCenter Drive, Suite 201
Milwaukee, Wisconsin 53212 USA

Series editor: Patricia Lantier-Sampon
Editorial assistants: Jamie Daniel, Diane Laska, Rita Reitci

Printed in the United States of America

1 2 3 4 5 6 7 8 9 99 98 97 96

CONTENTS

THE OCTOPUS'S WORLD

The octopus habitat

The octopus belongs to the scientific class Cephalopoda, which includes about 650 species of marine mollusks divided into forty-five families. All cephalopods alive today live in the sea, and fossils indicate they have always lived this way. Cephalopods live in all the oceans and in most of Earth's seas, from shallow waters to depths of over 23,000 feet (7,000 meters).

The octopus's appearance is unmistakable, with its enormous head and arms full of suckers.

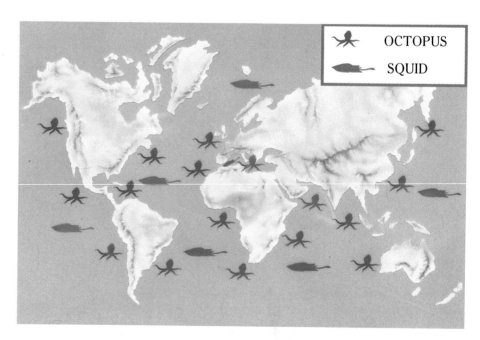

Cephalopods live in all the oceans, both in coastal areas and in the high seas.

Head over heels

The name *cephalopod* means "feet on one's head," and it describes one of this group's main characteristics. All cephalopods have a crown of muscular arms around the head, varying from ninety in the nautilus to eight in the octopus. If you have ever seen an octopus, you probably noticed only its arms and enormous head. This "head" is actually the main part of its body. It contains the respiratory and digestive systems and the heart.

A view from under the octopus's mouth, with its arms around it.

The octopus seems to have no body because its arms are directly below its head.

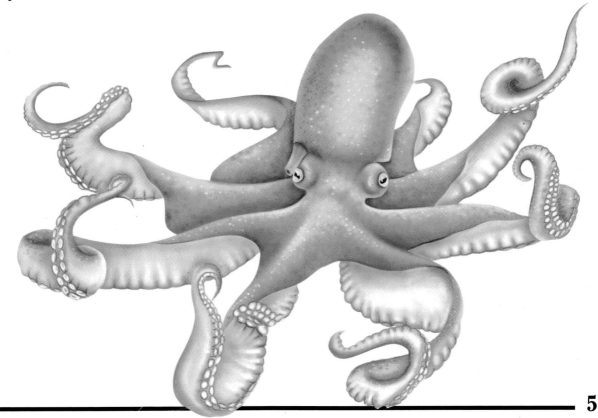

Types of cephalopods

The 650 species of cephalopods come in different shapes and sizes. Some only measure about .25 inches (6 mm) in length, while others can reach 66 feet (20 m) and weigh over one ton. The best-known cephalopods include the squid, the cuttlefish, and the octopus. All three are edible species. Cuttlefish and squid have ten limbs, made up of eight arms with suckers on their underside. They also have two longer arms that end in a large pad, which help capture

AUSTRALIAN SQUID — has luminescent organs.

SQUID

NAUTILUS — the only living cephalopod with an outside shell.

COMMON CUTTLEFISH

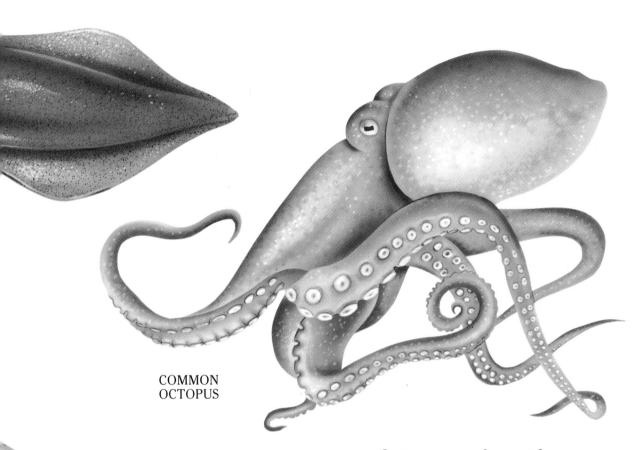

COMMON
OCTOPUS

prey. Octopuses do not have these two arms. They have only eight arms exactly the same length; for this reason, they are also called octopods. Lifestyles vary according to the species; octopuses usually spend most of their lives on the seabed, but squids are active swimmers that can cover long distances during the day. Squids use their fins to swim, although they also have a jet-propelled system similar to the octopus.

INSIDE THE OCTOPUS

The common octopus is an intelligent, curious animal. If you look at one up close, you can see its enormous head with two big eyes and the opening for the siphon. The body surrounds the head, from which stem the long arms with suckers. The common octopus can measure up to 3.3 feet (1 m) in length, and it can reach up to 33 pounds (15 kilograms) in weight. Some octopus species, however, can measure up to 30 feet (9 m) and weigh 550 pounds (250 kg).

CARTILAGINOUS HEAD CAPSULE
Surrounds and protects the brain like a skull (octopuses are invertebrates and have no bones).

EYES
Eyes are large and similar in structure to human eyes. The octopus can see clearly below the water.

BRAIN

PARROT BEAK
The octopus's mouth is shaped like a parrot's beak placed upside-down. With the powerful muscles that surround it, the beak has a strong bite.

SUCKERS
Each sucker has two rings of muscle that allow it to contract and stick to a surface.

FIRST RIGHT ARM

FIRST LEFT ARM

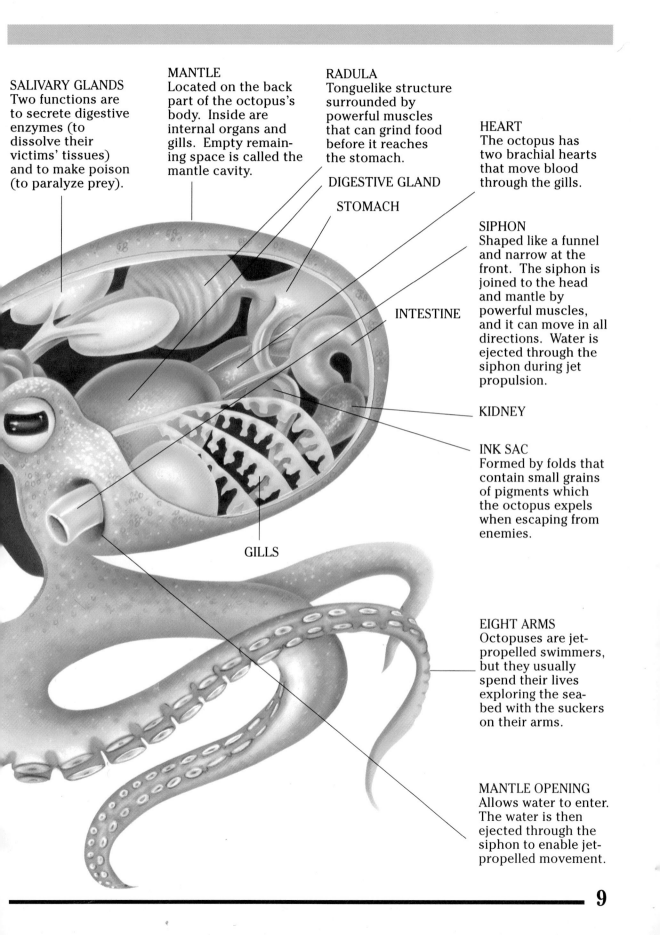

SALIVARY GLANDS
Two functions are to secrete digestive enzymes (to dissolve their victims' tissues) and to make poison (to paralyze prey).

MANTLE
Located on the back part of the octopus's body. Inside are internal organs and gills. Empty remaining space is called the mantle cavity.

RADULA
Tonguelike structure surrounded by powerful muscles that can grind food before it reaches the stomach.

DIGESTIVE GLAND

STOMACH

HEART
The octopus has two brachial hearts that move blood through the gills.

SIPHON
Shaped like a funnel and narrow at the front. The siphon is joined to the head and mantle by powerful muscles, and it can move in all directions. Water is ejected through the siphon during jet propulsion.

INTESTINE

KIDNEY

INK SAC
Formed by folds that contain small grains of pigments which the octopus expels when escaping from enemies.

GILLS

EIGHT ARMS
Octopuses are jet-propelled swimmers, but they usually spend their lives exploring the sea-bed with the suckers on their arms.

MANTLE OPENING
Allows water to enter. The water is then ejected through the siphon to enable jet-propelled movement.

JET-PROPELLED MOVEMENT

Ingenious locomotion

Soft-bodied animals often lack the muscle power needed to swim rapidly for long periods of time. Cephalopods are a spectacular exception, since they can swim as fast as most fish. They have developed an ingenious system of jet-propelled movement that allows them to travel quickly over long distances. One type of Japanese squid migrates over 1,245 miles (2,000 km), swimming nonstop for two and a half months.

The octopus moves on the seabed, walking on its arms and clinging to the bottom using its rows of suckers.

The octopus uses jet-propelled action to move quickly.

that octopuses can change color instantly?

Octopuses can change color gradually or in an instant because their nervous system controls their skin pigment. Colored pigment is located inside cells called chromatophores, which are surrounded by rings of muscle fiber. When they receive a stimulus, the tiny muscles tense, and the pigment forms stains on the body. Octopuses can assume different colors by combining blue, pink, black, brown, and purple pigments.

Bursts of speed

Octopuses, and cephalopods in general, can move quickly because of their ingenious jet-propelled system of locomotion.

To do this, they draw water into the mantle cavity, then eject the water at high pressure through a siphon. This technique allows the animals to develop bursts of speed to escape their enemies. The jet of water propels them to safety.

Some species of very small squid can propel themselves forward to a distance equal to 25 times the length of their body

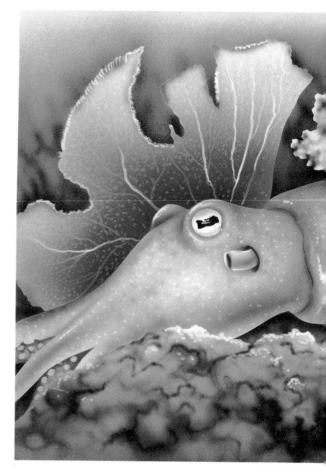

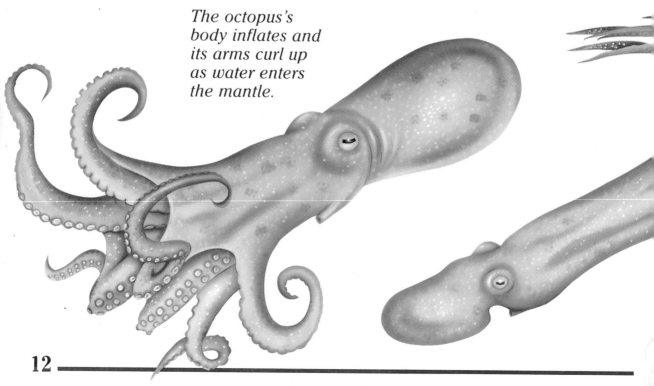

The octopus's body inflates and its arms curl up as water enters the mantle.

The octopus usually prefers to stay hidden, camouflaged among the rocks on the seabed.

in one second. Imagine a human swimming over 150 feet (45 m) in one second! Some cephalopods can even reach top speeds of 45 miles (72 km) per hour. However, they cannot keep up this effort for any length of time.

Some species can jump as far as 165 feet (50 m) over the water and can reach heights of 13 feet (4 m) above the surface. This is useful when the octopus must escape from its enemies. After the cephalopod's impressive burst of speed, the pursuers are often unable to guess where their "lunch" has gone.

Many squid travel in large schools that rise to the water's surface at night.

Its body stretches to a maximum while water is expelled from the siphon.

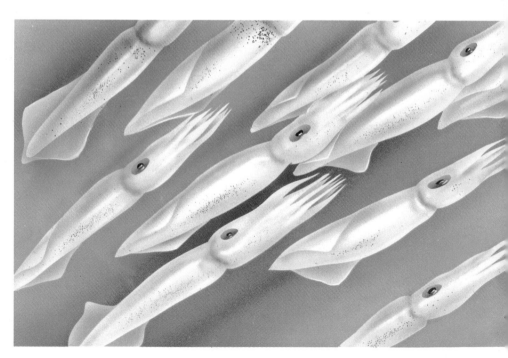

SWIMMING WITH MANY ARMS

How does jet propulsion work?

Jet-propelled movement is a cyclic process with two phases. First, water is pulled into the mantle cavity. During this time, the siphon remains closed. Second, the water that has just entered is then ejected back to the outside through the flexible siphon while the mantle opening remains closed. This inward and outward pumping of water is accomplished through

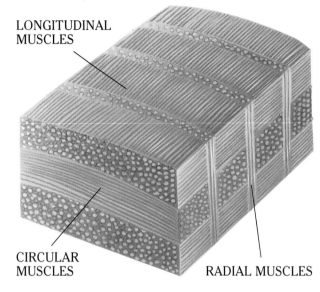

LONGITUDINAL MUSCLES

CIRCULAR MUSCLES

RADIAL MUSCLES

Circular muscles in the mantle contract it to create the jet of water.

The octopus catches prey with its arms.

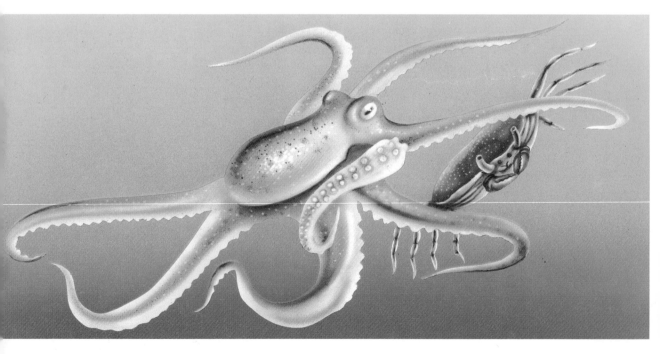

alternate contractions of the muscles in the mantle. For this system of locomotion to work properly, muscle activity must be exactly and perfectly coordinated. This requires special nerve control. Cephalopods have strong muscles that enable the mantle to contract as needed. The disadvantage of jet-propelled movement is that it requires a huge amount of energy from the animals.

While the octopus rests, its arm suckers explore every corner of the seabed.

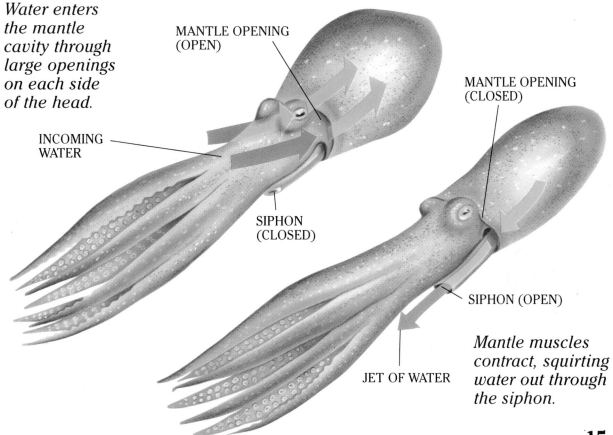

Water enters the mantle cavity through large openings on each side of the head.

MANTLE OPENING (OPEN)

MANTLE OPENING (CLOSED)

INCOMING WATER

SIPHON (CLOSED)

SIPHON (OPEN)

JET OF WATER

Mantle muscles contract, squirting water out through the siphon.

that the octopus's mouth is shaped like a parrot's beak?

Octopuses use their arms to catch prey — crustaceans, fish, and other mollusks. After the prey is trapped, the octopus opens its two strong, horny jaws, similar to a parrot's beak but upside-down. The octopus then paralyzes its victims by injecting a poison produced by its salivary glands. It covers the prey with digestive juices that partly dissolve the prey's tissues.

Octopus ink!

The octopus has a special gland and sac of ink near the anal opening. The ink is a thick, black liquid that spreads quickly in the water (some deep-water cephalopods emit a luminous ink). The ink also contains a substance that irritates predators' eyes and paralyzes their sense of smell for a few seconds. The ink is a defense mechanism for the octopus that hides and protects it while it escapes.

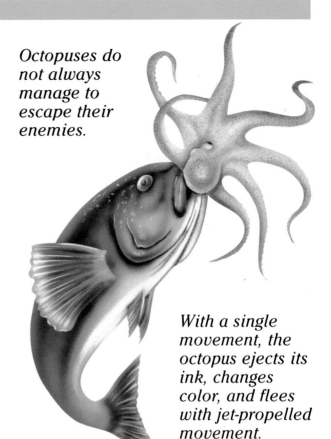

Octopuses do not always manage to escape their enemies.

With a single movement, the octopus ejects its ink, changes color, and flees with jet-propelled movement.

OCTOPUS ANCESTORS

Armored cephalopods

The first cephalopods appeared over 500 million years ago. Although present forms have no outside shell, fossils of primitive cephalopods show giant, conical shells 15 feet (4.5 m) in length with a 12-inch (30-cm) opening. Pachydiscus, which lived 300 million years ago, had the largest shell — over 10 feet (3 m) wide. Ancestors of modern octopuses first appeared at the end of the Paleozoic Era, 240 million years ago.

Nautiloid shells over 15 feet (4.5 m) long have been discovered.

that the giant squid is the largest invertebrate ever?

The largest invertebrate that exists or has ever existed is Architeuthis, or the giant squid. It lives in the deepest oceans and rarely rises to the surface. It can measure more than 60 feet (18 m) in length and 16 feet (5 m) in diameter and weigh more than one ton. Sperm whales will descend more than 3,280 feet (1,000 m) to hunt them, but huge squids are capable of drowning their enemies by holding onto them with their tentacles.

Nautilus: a living fossil

Over 350 million years ago, nautiloid forms (or ammonites) already existed in the oceans. They were almost identical to the present-day Nautilus, although they were larger; some measured over 6.5 feet (2 m) in diameter. The shell of the Nautilus now rarely measures more than 12 inches (30 cm) in diameter. There are presently about half a dozen species of Nautilus in the tropical seas; they feed on small fish that they trap with their tentacles.

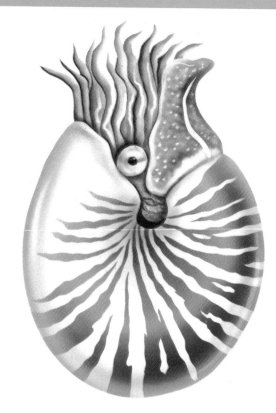

Some species of Nautilus have up to ninety tentacles.

The primitive Nautilus of over 300 million years ago is similar in appearance to modern species.

THE LIFE OF THE OCTOPUS

Curious and intelligent

Octopuses are curious and intelligent invertebrates. Like humans, they possess short-term and long-term memory. They also have two different learning systems: one is based on sight (visual), and the other on touch (tactile). The octopus solves problems with the help of past experience. When it solves a problem, it remembers, and from then on solves similar problems in the same way.

The octopus explores everything with its suckers, which send detailed and precise messages to the brain.

The octopus brain has fifteen pairs of lobes that receive information to control and guide its body parts.

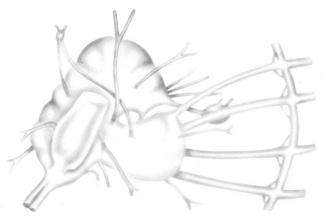

A lateral, or side, view of the octopus's brain.

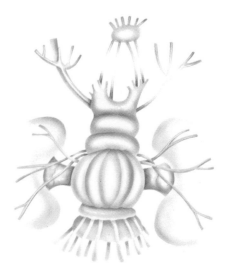

A dorsal, or top, view of the octopus's brain.

Perfect sight

Cephalopods have highly developed sensory systems, and this is especially true of their eyes. The octopus has two large eyes that can form clear images in the water. Octopuses depend on their sight to catch prey and detect enemies, and they have an almost 360° field of vision. Octopus eyes are similar to human eyes. Each eye has an eyelid, an iris, crystalline lens, and a retina that receives focused images.

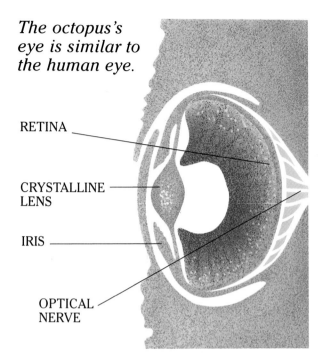

The octopus's eye is similar to the human eye.

RETINA

CRYSTALLINE LENS

IRIS

OPTICAL NERVE

The eyes, located just outside of the mantle, have a 360° field of vision capacity.

Youngsters by the thousands

After mating, the female octopus retreats to a hiding place among the rocks to lay eggs and wait for them to hatch. The number of eggs varies greatly from species to species, from a few dozen to hundreds of thousands. The female takes good care of the eggs — protecting them from predators, cleaning them with its suckers, and providing them with oxygen by squirting jets of water. While the female incubates the eggs, it stops eating, weakens, and dies after the birth of the babies.

The female octopus can touch and care for the delicate eggs without breaking them.

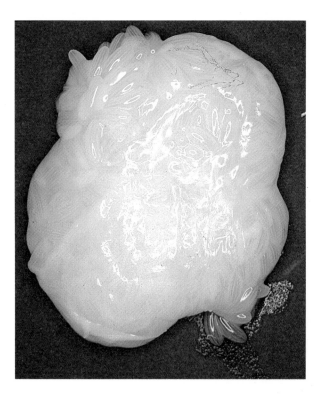

Egg masses look jelly-like because of their high liquid content.

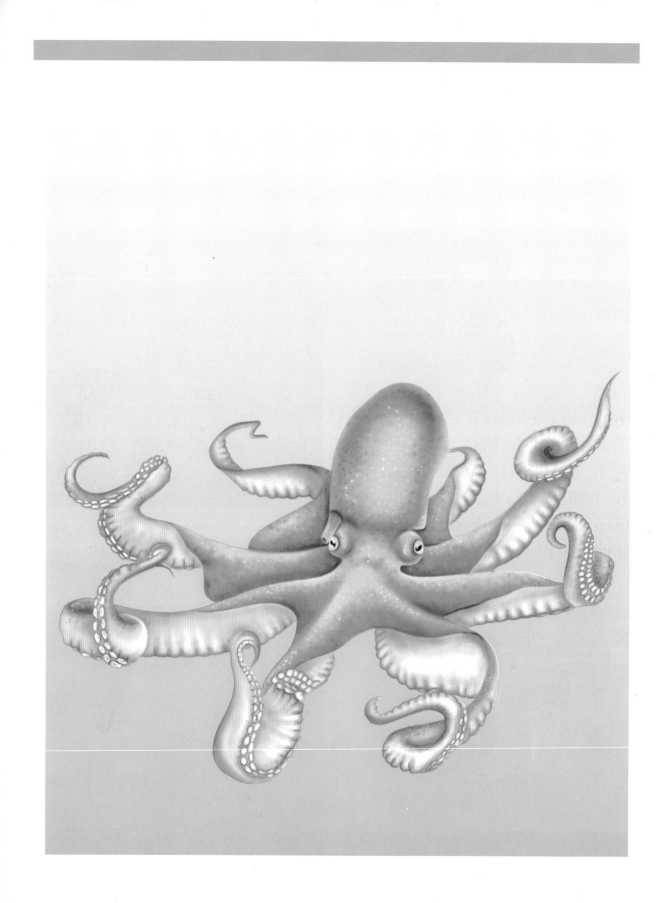

APPENDIX TO

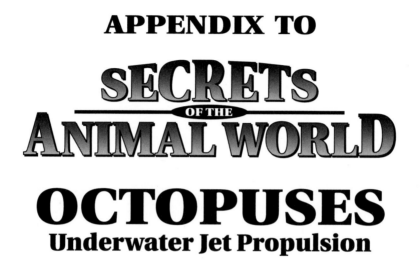

OCTOPUSES
Underwater Jet Propulsion

OCTOPUS SECRETS

▼ **An octopus with a shell.**
The female Paper Nautilus carries a hard capsule lined with mother-of-pearl that it uses to transport and incubate eggs.

▼ **A very appetizing animal.**
Cephalopods are a good food source for humans. Over 2.2 million tons (2 million metric tons) are caught every year, or 2 percent of all food extracted from the sea.

Spare arms. Cephalopods can regenerate, or regrow, certain parts of their body, although they may be weaker or deformed.

Very prolific parents. Of the 200,000 young that an octopus can have, very few survive the first hours. Many fish wait for the eggs to hatch to devour them. In most cases, only one or two young will reach adulthood and reproduce.

Slower than fish. Octopuses pump a high volume of blood per time unit for their system of jet propulsion: they need eight times more blood than fish to move at half the speed.

Monster squids. About 100 years ago, a squid caught in the Atlantic Ocean measured about 50 feet (15 m) in length without counting its tentacles, and weighed over 2 tons.

▶ **A very short life.** Most cephalopods have a very short life. The life cycle of small species lasts between five and six months. Only the larger species or those living in cold waters manage to live for five years.

1. Octopuses, squids, and cuttlefish belong to the class:
   a) Octopods.
   b) Invertebrate Pulphopods.
   c) Cephalopoda.

2. What is the cephalopod's maximum speed?
   a) 45 miles per hour (72 kmph).
   b) 160 miles per hour (257 kmph).
   c) 116 miles per hour (186 kmph).

3. How many species of cephalopods exist?
   a) 13,250.
   b) 57.
   c) 650.

4. The largest invertebrate ever to have existed is:
   a) Gigantoteutis.
   b) Architeuthis.
   c) Enorminverteus.

5. Through jet-propulsion, the octopus expels water through:
   a) the mantle openings.
   b) the anus.
   c) the siphon.

6. How many arms does an octopus have?
   a) eight.
   b) ten.
   c) two.

The answers to OCTOPUS SECRETS questions are on page 32.

GLOSSARY

ammonites: fossil shells of ammonoids — cephalopod mollusks from the Paleozoic and Mesozoic eras, now extinct.

ancestors: previous generations; predecessors.

camouflage: a way of disguising something or someone to make it look like its surroundings.

capsule: a small container or compartment.

cells: the smallest, most basic parts of plants and animals.

cephalopods: mollusks that have arms attached to their heads, such as squid and octopuses.

chromatophores: cells containing pigments that produce a temporary color, often to help provide camouflage.

crustaceans: animals with segmented bodies and a hard outer shell that live mostly in water. Lobsters, shrimp, and crabs are crustaceans.

devour: to eat hungrily and greedily.

digestive system: an organism's internal system that works to pass food from the mouth to the organs that break it down into nutrients. The body uses what it needs and then sends the rest out as waste.

dorsal: referring to the back, or topmost part of an organ or an animal in its normal position.

edible: capable of being eaten.

eject: to throw out by force.

expel: to force out.

fins: thin, flat parts that stick out from the body of a water animal. Fins are used by the animal for steering and balance.

flexible: able to bend or move with ease. Octopus arms are muscular and flexible.

fossil: traces or remains of plants and animals from an earlier time found in rock.

glands: organs in the body that make and release substances such as sweat, tears, and saliva. Octopus salivary glands release poison to paralyze prey and enzymes to digest it.

habitat: the natural home of a plant or animal.

incubate: to keep eggs warm, usually with body heat, so they will hatch.

inflate: to fill with air or gas and expand.

ingenious: clever, creative.

invertebrates: animals that have no backbone.

iris: the colored part of the eye.

jet propulsion: the way a body can push itself in a forward direction by ejecting a liquid or gas.

lateral: referring to the side of an organ or an animal when it is in its normal position.

locomotion: the act of moving from one place to another.

longitudinal: running along the length of something.

luminous: shining; giving off light.

marine: of or related to the sea.

mate (v): to join together (animals) to produce young.

migrate: to move from one place or climate to another, usually on a seasonal basis.

mollusks: invertebrate animals, such as snails and clams, that usually live in water and have hard outer shells.

paralyze: to cause something or someone to be unable to move or function normally.

pigment: a substance in plants or animals that gives them color.

predators: animals that kill and eat other animals.

prey: animals that are hunted, captured, and killed by other animals for food.

primitive: of or relating to an early and usually simple stage of development.

prolific: able to reproduce in great numbers.

regenerate: to renew or restore to original strength or health.

respiratory system: the system of air passages through which a living thing breathes.

retina: a lining on the inside of the eyeball that is sensitive to light.

The retina is connected to the brain by the optic nerve and carries images formed by the lens to the brain.

saliva: the fluid made by glands in the mouth to keep the mouth moist and to help in chewing, swallowing, and digesting food.

species: animals or plants that are closely related and often similar in behavior and appearance. Members of the same species can breed together.

stimulus: something that causes a reaction or movement.

tactile: related to or perceived through the sense of touch.

tentacles: flexible, armlike body parts that certain animals use for moving around and catching prey.

tropical: belonging to the tropics, or the region centered on the equator and lying between the Tropic of Cancer (23.5 degrees north of the equator) and the Tropic of Capricorn (23.5 degrees south of the equator). This region is typically very hot and humid.

ACTIVITIES

◆ Do you live near a seashore, river, or lake? If so, find out all you can about what creatures live in the water. Are there any mollusks? What about crustaceans and other creatures with shells? Make a journal recording everything you find out by going to the library and by observing for yourself.

◆ If you can visit an aquarium, spend some time observing the octopuses or other cephalopods there. Find out what they are fed, and how their behavior changes in captivity.

◆ Many cephalopod habitats are being threatened by water pollution and other human activities. Read all you can about the effects of water pollution on marine life. Which of these cephalopods do humans use as food? What can you and your friends and family do to reduce the harmful effects on these valuable resources?

MORE BOOKS TO READ

Deep Sea Vents: Living Worlds Without Sun. John F. Waters (Dutton)
Down in the Sea: The Octopus. Patricia Kite (A. Whitman)
Dying Oceans. Paula Hogan (Gareth Stevens)
Exploring Salt Water Habitats. Sue Smith (Mondo)
Great Barrier Reef. Martin J. Gutnik and Natalie Browne-Gutnik
    (Raintree Steck-Vaughn)
The Living Ocean. Elizabeth Collins (Chelsea House)
Octopuses. Jenny Markert (Childs World)
Safari Beneath the Sea: The Wonder World of the North Pacific
    Diane Swanson (Sierra Books)
Secrets of the Deep. Ingrid Selberg (Dial Books)
You Can Be a Woman Marine Biologist. Florence McClary and
    Judith L. Cohen (Cascade)

VIDEOS

Life on Earth: The Conquest of the Waters. (John D. and Catherine T.
    MacArthur Foundation Library)
The Octopus. Animal Family series. (Barr films)
Octopus, Octopus. Undersea World of Jacques Cousteau series.
    (Churchill Media)

PLACES TO VISIT

The Marine Life Center
1200 U. S. Highway 1
Loggerhead Park
Juno Beach, FL 33408

The Shedd Aquarium
Roosevelt Road at
    Lakeshore Drive
Chicago IL 60605

The Montreal Aquarium
La Ronde, Île Ste-Helene
Montreal, Quebec
H3C 1A0

Sydney Aquarium
Wheat Road
Pier 26
Darling Harbour
Sydney, Australia

The Vancouver Aquarium
In Stanley Park
P.O. Box 3232
Vancouver, British
    Columbia V6B 3X8

**Kelly Tarlton's
    Underwater World**
23 Tamaki Drive
Auckland, New Zealand

INDEX

Answers to OCTOPUS SECRETS questions:
1. c
2. a
3. c
4. b
5. c
6. a